PTQ TUITION **NEW TRANSFER TESTS**

MULTIPLE-CHOICE

ENGLISH

Practice Test 7

Guidance for completing this Test

1. Read the passages carefully.

2. Read the questions thoroughly.

3. Read the answers carefully.

4. Choose what you think is the correct answer carefully.

5. Underline or circle the answer, immediately after the question.

6. Transfer the LETTER **A,B,C,D,E** or **N** to the answer sheet.

7. Make sure to mark the answer box like [—] not [✓].

8. Check carefully that you have transferred your correct answer.

9 . This test lasts for **50 minutes.**

PUPIL'S NAME _____

TOTAL MARK
(Out of 60)

Read this passage and answer the questions which follow. If there are any words you don't understand you may find them in the Glossary at the end of the test.

THE BAKING PROCESS

1.   **Baking** is the technique of prolonged cooking of food by dry heat acting by convection, normally in an oven, but also in hot ashes, or on hot stones. It is primarily used for the preparation of bread, cakes, pastries and pies, tarts, quiches,
5.   and cookies. Such items are sometimes referred to as "baked goods," and are sold at a bakery.
        A person who prepares baked goods as a profession is called a baker. Baking is also used for the preparation of baked potatoes, baked apples, baked beans, some pasta dishes such
10.   as lasagne, and various other foods, such as the pretzel.
        Many commercial ovens are provided with two heating elements: one for baking, using convection and conduction to heat the food, and one for broiling or grilling, heating mainly by radiation. Meat may be baked, but is more often roasted, a
15.   similar process, using higher temperatures and shorter cooking times.
        The baking process does not add any fat to the product, and producers of snack products such as potato chips are also beginning to replace the process of deep-frying with baking
20.   in order to reduce the fat content of their products.
        The dry heat of baking changes the form of starches in the food and causes its outer surfaces to brown, giving it an attractive appearance and taste, while partially sealing in the food's moisture. The browning is caused by caramelization
25.   of sugars and the Maillard reaction. Moisture is never really entirely "sealed in", however; over time, an item being baked will become dry. This is often an advantage, especially in situations where drying is the desired outcome, for example, in drying herbs or in roasting certain types of vegetables.
30.   The most common baked item is bread. Variations in the ovens, ingredients and recipes used in the baking of bread result in the wide variety of breads produced around the world. Some foods are surrounded with moisture during baking by placing a small amount of liquid (such as water
35.   or broth) in the bottom of a closed pan, and letting it steam up around the food, a method commonly known as braising or slow baking.
        When baking, consideration must be given to the amount   1.
of fat that is contained in the food item. Higher levels of fat such

40. as margarine, butter or vegetable shortening will cause an item
     to spread out during the baking process.
          With the passage of time breads harden; they become stale.
     This is not primarily due to moisture being lost from the baked
     products, but more a reorganization of the way in which the water
45. and starch are associated over time. This process is similar to
     recrystallization, and is promoted by storage at cool temperatures,
     such as in a domestic refrigerator.

**Answer the following questions. Look back over the passage.
You should choose the _best_ answer and mark its letter on
your answer sheet.**

1. What are usually referred to as **"baked goods"** ?

A.   ...supermarket items.   B.   ...food made in a bakery.
C.   ...butchers' products.   D.   ...items in a greengrocers.
E.   ...the ingredients for bread.

2. The outcome of adding higher levels of fat when baking is

A.   ...the bread tastes better and smoother.
B.   ...the bread will stay fresh longer.
C.   ...the baked item will spread out.
D.   ...less flour is needed for the baked item.
E.   ...less liquid is needed for the baked item.

3. The process which ensures the least amount of fat in
    cooked items is

A.   ...broiling   B.   ...grilling
C.   ...deep-frying   D.   ...baking
E.   ...roasting

4. The main sources of fat for baking are

A.   ...oil and milk.   B.   ...butter and margarine.
C.   ...beans and pasta.   D.   ...apples and potatoes.
E.   ...vegetables and broth.

5. A baking element and broiling/grilling element are found in

A.   ...domestic cookers.   B.   ...commercial ovens.
C.   ...deep-fat frier.   D.   ...a microwave oven.
E.   ...domestic refrigerator.

2.

6.   Bread can be baked

A.   ...on hot stones.
B.   ...in a freezer.
C.   ...on the kitchen table.
D.   ...in a deep-fat frier.
E.   ...in a closed pan with water.

7.   The food's moisture is partially sealed in

A.   ...when extra fat is added to the baking mixture.
B.   ...when the heat of the oven is at its maximum.
C.   ...when the item to be baked is placed at the bottom of the oven
D.   ...when the baking changes the form of the starches in the food.
E.   ...when the baking results in the product being dried.

8.   The **"browning"** on the outer surfaces of bread is caused by

A.   ...too much heat
B.   ...too much fat
C.   ...too much moisture
D.   ...the caramelisation of sugars
E.   ...too much flour

9.   Braising or slow baking is achieved

A.   ...by having a low oven temperature.
B.   ...by having a high oven temperature.
C.   ...by letting moisture steam up around the food.
D.   ...by using shorter baking times.
E.   ...by using longer baking time.

10.   Besides bread other foods that are cooked by means of baking are

A.   ...pasta dishes and potatoes.
B.   ...beans and peas.
C.   ...porridge and apples.
D.   ...pretzel and onions.
E.   ...butter and margarine.

The following passage contains a number of mistakes. You have to find the mistakes. On each line there is either _one_ mistake or _no_ mistake. Find the group of words in which there is a mistake and mark the letter for it on your answer sheet. If there is no mistake, mark N.

First, look for the _spelling_ mistakes.

11. The Rowan / family decided / to visit their / nearer sea-side
    A   B   C   D   N

12. resort and / they prepared / a picnik to take / with them. When
    A   B   C   D   N

13. they arrived / the father was / appaled by what / he came across.
    A   B   C   D   N

14. Not only was / the appearance / very untidy / but the entire
    A   B   C   D   N

15. surroundings / presented a / dangerous / health hasard.
    A   B   C   D   N

16. The beech / was littered with / empty glass bottles, / half-empty
    A   B   C   D   N

17. drinks cans, / discared newspapers / and magazines / and the
    A   B   C   D   N

18. remains of / items of clothing / and footwere as / well as food.
    A   B   C   D   N

19. In addition to / all the rubish / the people / were allowing
    A   B   C   D   N

20. their dogs to / run around / and releive themselves / on the sand.
    A   B   C   D   N

Now look for _punctuation_ mistakes.

21. "Where are we / going to park / our car, Daddy ! " / daughter
    A   B   C   D   N

22. Amy asked. / Daddy s response / was to throw / his hands up
    A   B   C   D   N

4.

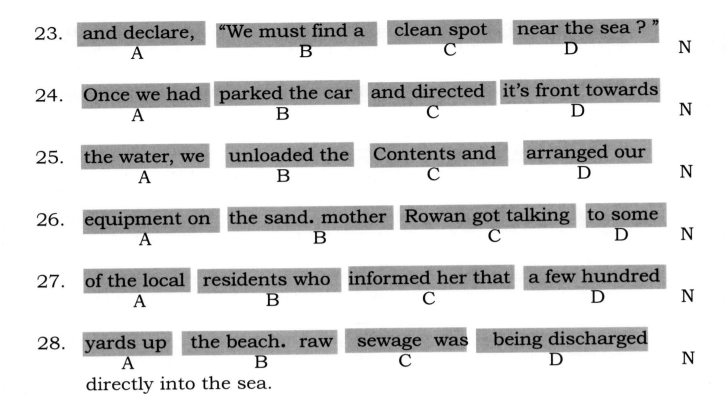

23. and declare, "We must find a clean spot near the sea ?"
    A   B   C   D   N

24. Once we had parked the car and directed it's front towards
    A   B   C   D   N

25. the water, we unloaded the Contents and arranged our
    A   B   C   D   N

26. equipment on the sand. mother Rowan got talking to some
    A   B   C   D   N

27. of the local residents who informed her that a few hundred
    A   B   C   D   N

28. yards up the beach. raw sewage was being discharged
    A   B   C   D   N

directly into the sea.

**Read this passage and answer the questions which follow.
If there are any words you don't understand you may find
them in the Glossary at the end of the test.**

FAMILY OF NINE

1.   Simon jumped as he heard a horn and a Land Rover
     drove onto the dock, full of children who kept piling out, like
     clowns out of a car at a circus. It was difficult to keep count
     but Simon managed to determine that there was a mother
5.   and father and seven children.
        After considerable laughing and shouting, the two older
     children, a boy and a girl, got themselves organised and managed
     to pull two suitcases from the Land Rover. The two of them came
     to stand just beside Simon. The mother urged the younger
10. children back into the vehicle, out of the rain and the father,
     rain dripping off his hat, stood leaning on the window,
     talking to the mother.
        The girl was carrying her suitcase as it banged against
     her knees and deposited it beside the gangplank. She then
15. proceeded towards Simon as her brother followed in her wake.
     Simon reckoned that the girl was a year older than him, about
     fourteen years old, so he felt that she would resent being called a
     child. Her brother would have been about twelve years old, even
     though he was as tall as Simon. Both brother and sister wore
20. waterproof clothing and were considerably drier than Simon,
     whose fair hair was slicked wetly to his head.

"Hello," the girl said. "Are you going on the Orion ?"
Her accent was not quite foreign but it was certainly more precise
than the soft Southern speech Simon was accustomed to hearing.
25.   "Yes, I am. Are you ?"
"Yes. At least, Charles and Daddy and I will be going."
As she made this reply she smiled, a smile spreading like
sunshine across her face. Then she remarked, "How nice to
have someone our age. Daddy warned us that freighter
30. passengers are usually ancient. I'm Poly O'Keefe, pronounced
Polly but spelt with one l. I'm fourteen and this is my brother,
Charles, who is twelve."
        Simon was correct. "I'm Simon Renier and I'm thirteen.
Again Poly smiled, a shaft of light lifting the gloom of the day.
35.   "You're not travelling alone, are you ?"
Simon pointed to the man and the old woman. Suddenly
cousin Forsyth stepped forward as one of the fork lifts picked
up a large flat wooden crate. His cousin watched anxiously as ropes
were looped over it and fussed, "Be careful. It's extremely
40. valuable as it contains an irreplaceable portrait."
        Dock hands nodded in an indifferent manner as they
continued their business. The fork lift backed away from the
crate which was then lifted up in the air and hung swinging
between the dock and the freighter. Simon watched the crate and
45. also kept an eye on his cousin as the special crate was slowly
lowered safely onto the ship's deck. Reaction from cousin
Forsyth was one of comfort.

29. What is unusual about the girl's name ?

A.   It sounds like an Irish name.   B.   Simon made fun of it.
C.   It has one less letter than usual. D.   It is very short.
E.   It sounded like a boy's name.

30. Simon jumped

A.   ...when the crate was picked up by the fork lifts.
B.   ...when the crate crashed onto the deck.
C.   ...when cousin Forsyth stepped forward.
D.   ...when seven children poured out of the Land Rover.
E.   ...when the horn of the Land Rover was sounded.

31. The Orion is described as

A.   a circus.   B.   a vehicle.   C.   a freighter.
D.   a ship.   E.   a gangplank.

6.

32.   The girl's smile is compared to

A.   sunshine / shaft of light   B.   laughing / shouting
C.   drier / fair   D.   spreading / soft
E.   foreign / clownlike

33.   The phrase in **line 23**, **"her accent was not quite foreign"** means

A.   ...she spoke exactly like her fellow citizens.
B.   ...she spoke in a very strange voice.
C.   ...her speech was similar to foreign people.
D.   ...the manner of her speech wasn't exactly alien.
E.   ...it was difficult to understand the way she talked.

34.   The children's exit from the Land Rover is described as

A.   a circus.   B.   organised and managed
C.   laughing and shouting   D.   dripping with water
E.   emptying out like clowns.

35.   Why would Poly **resent being called a child (line 17/18)** ?

A.   ...she was laughing and shouting.
B.   ...she was fourteen years old.
C.   ...she was behaving like a clown.
D.   ...she was the eldest.
E.   ...Simon had called her a child.

36.   What colour was Simon's hair ?

A.   brown   B.   fair   C.   ginger
D.   black   E.   dark

37.   What was Forsyth's emotion in the **last paragraph** ?

A.   alarm   B.   anger   C.   indifference
D.   relief   E.   delight

38.   The portrait was valuable because

A.   ...it was in a wooden crate.   B.   ...it belonged to Forsyth.
C.   ...it couldn't be replaced   D.   ...it was of his aunt.
E.   ...it had cost a lot of money.

39. The phrase in **line 15**, **"followed in her wake "** has the same meaning as

A. ...walked by her side.
B. ...stumbled after her.
C. ...took the same path as her.
D. ...proceeded to sleepwalk after her.
E. ...walked in the opposite direction.

40. The best meaning for **"indifferent manner"** as used in **line 41** is

A. unconcerned behaviour   B. conscientious behaviour
C. bad manners   D. not the same as normal
E. very appropriate

41. Which words in the **last paragraph** are Proper nouns ?

A. Dock / manner   B. his / their
C. Reaction / cousin   D. Simon / Forsyth
E. comfort / business

42. Which word in the **third paragraph** (from **line 13 to line 21**) means **set down** ?

A. resent   B. proceeded   C. followed
D. deposited   E. slicked

**Read this passage and answer the questions which follow.
If there are any words you don't understand you may find them
in the Glossary at the end of the test.**

FLORENCE FROM A WINDOW

1.   It was nice to wake up in Florence, to view with open eyes a bright bare room, with a floor of red tiles which looked clean though they were not. It had a painted ceiling upon which pink griffins and blue amorini ramble among a group of bassoons and

5. violins. It was also pleasant to fling open the windows to lean out into sunshine with beautiful hills and trees and marble churches opposite and nearby the River Arno, gurgling against the embankment of the road.

     Across the river men were at work with spades and sieves on

10. the sandy foreshore and on the river was a boat, also employed for some mysterious purpose. An electric tram came rushing underneath the window. Except for one tourist there were no passengers seated but its platforms were overflowing with Italians, who preferred to stand.

15.   Children were trying to hang on to the tram and the conductor, with no malice, spat in their faces to make them let go. Then soldiers appeared, good-looking, undersized men, each wearing a knapsack covered with mangy fur, and a great-coat which had been cut for some larger soldier. Behind them walked

20.   officers, looking fierce and foolish, and then came prancing, little boys, turning somersaults in time with the band.

       The tramcar became entangled in their ranks and moved on painfully like a caterpillar in a swarm of ants. One of the little somersaulting boys fell over and some white bullocks came

25.   out of an alleyway. Indeed, if it hadn't been for the good advice of an old man who was selling buttons and hooks, the road might never have been cleared.

       He had seen the imminent danger and had already moved with surprising agility across in front of the officers. He grabbed

30.   the little boy who had fallen but he was not seriously hurt. It was only his pride that had suffered with his fellow somersaulters seeing him incapable of completing the movements.

       The old man made sure that the boy was alright because he couldn't stop him from joining his mates and continuing to carry

35.   out his duties as one of the entertainments. As the bustle of the day passed the open window there was a knock on the door and Miss Bartlett entered, since it was always left unlocked.

       The occupant of the room, Lucy, welcomed her cousin who was already prepared for the day and by the time Lucy

40.   had got dressed her cousin, Miss Bartlett had made her breakfast. A conversation then ensued on not unfamiliar lines. As Miss Bartlett was somewhat tired she thought they had better spend the morning in but Lucy was adamant that it was her first day in Florence and she would prefer to go out and soak

45.   up the atmosphere of this famous city. So she could go alone but Miss Bartlett wouldn't have this, saying that she would accompany Lucy anywhere she wished to go.

43.   Which of the following is the correct order in which the characters appear in the third paragraph ?

A.   conductor, children, soldiers, little boys, officers.
B.   little boys, officers, soldiers, children, conductor.
C.   children, conductor, soldiers, officers, little boys.
D.   soldiers, officers, children, conductor, little boys.
E.   officers, soldiers, conductor, little boys, children.

44. The pink griffins and the blue amorini rambled

A. ...in the garden.
C. ...in the street.
E. ...on the churches.

B. ...on the ceiling.
D. ...on the walls.

45. What are the men across the river using in their work ?

A. a boat and a tram.
C. sieves and spades.
E. bassoons and violins.

B. a digger and lorry.
D. shovels and rakes.

46. What is compared to a **"caterpillar in a swarm of ants"** ?

A. the tramcar.
C. the boat.
E. the somersaulting boys.

B. the train.
D. the soldiers.

47. The children were treated in a nasty way by

A. the workmen.
C. the soldiers.
E. the conductor.

B. the officers.
D. the swarm of ants.

48. In the last paragraph Lucy and Miss Bartlett disagreed about

A. ...who would make breakfast.
B. ...who would go out to buy groceries.
C. ...when they would get dressed.
D. ...whether Lucy should go out alone.
E. ...whether Miss Bartlett should go out alone.

49. When the little boy fell the only thing that he hurt was

A. his wrist.
C. his leg.
E. his confidence.

B. his pride.
D. his head.

10.

50.   The soldiers were wearing

A.   boots and leggings.   B.   knapsack and outsized coat.
C.   coat and fur.   D.   fur coats and bags.
E.   helmets and belts.

51.   The best description of the Florence room is

A.   ...dull, well furnished, carpeted floor, tiled ceiling.
B.   ...bright, walls covered with paintings, bare floor, lighted ceiling.
C.   ...painted ceiling, tiled floor, bare, bright.
D.   ...dull ceiling, wooden floor, unfurnished, drab.
E.   ...painted floor, tiled walls, bright, decorated ceiling.

52.   The somersaulting boy who fell was in danger of being trampled by

A.   the officers and bullocks.   B.   the tram and the workmen.
C.   the soldiers and the old man. D.   the band and Lucy.
E.   the Italians and the tourist.

53.   What is meant by the expression, **"on not unfamiliar lines"**
      in **line 41** ?

A.   in an unusual way.   B.   in a strange way.
C.   in a different way.   D.   with a difficult method.
E.   in an accustomed manner.

54.   The most appropriate meaning for the word **"malice"** as it is
      used in **line 16** is

A.   sorrow   B.   love   C.   ill will
D.   regret   E.   thought

55.   The **three nouns** in **line 10** are

A.   the, sandy, foreshore   B.   for, employed, also
C.   boat, was, river   D.   foreshore, river, boat
E.   sandy, employed, boat

General Section

To answer these questions, you may have to think about the passages you have read. Look back at these if you need to. Look also at the Index and Glossary.

56. (a) A publication which is usually produced each week and has cartoon-style pictures and words directed at children is

A. a magazine   B. a newspaper
C. a diary   D. a comic

(b). The best description of a newspaper is

A. ...a regular publication produced with glossy photos.
B. ...a short official report or announcement.
C. ...a publication in which you find word meanings.
D. ...published daily/weekly about news/sport/current affairs.

57. (a) The words in the Glossary which are associated with baking are

A. ...bassoons and conduction.   B. ...imminent and broiling.
C. ...ingredients and pretzel.   D. ...griffins and sieves.

(b). The section of the test in which you would find aspects of city life is

A. the INDEX   B. BAKING
C. the GLOSSARY   D. FLORENCE FROM A WINDOW

58. (a) The hyphenated word below is

A. son-in-law   B. playground
C. GRAMMAR   D. Margaret

(b). The two words below which could be described as **homonymns** are

A. litter and herd   B. board and bored
C. masculine and feminine   D. transparent and opaque

12.

59. (a) The sentence below in which a verb is used **incorrectly** is

A. The game had ended abruptly.
B. Last night the family enjoyed a barbecue.
C. Mary is dreaming about her visit to the zoo.
D. Yesterday the secretary written a letter to a client.

In each of the following questions you have to choose the best word or group of words to complete this passage so that it makes sense. Choose one of the answers and mark the letter on the answer sheet.

59. A circus had arrived in the town on a Saturday and set up their

(b). tent in a **sensible**   **suitable**   **serious**   **straight**   field in which
                  A   B   C   D

60. (a). **they're**   **their**   **there**   **these**   was a flat surface. The
          A   B   C   D

(b). expectation was that this would be the **more**   **less**   **little**   **most**
                                         A   B   C   D

exciting event to happen this year.

13.

GLOSSARY

technique-------	method or skill used for a particular job
convection------	heating in liquids by currents circling
pretzel----------	bread in the form of a three-looped knot
conduction-----	movement of heat or electricity
broiling---------	cooking by means of grilling
caramelization-	making sugar and milk into chewy sweet
ingredients-----	things used to make up a mixture as in cooking
gangplank------	portable bridge to get on or off ships
bassoons----------	woodwind musical instrument
sieves-----------	tool with mesh through which substances are sifted
conductor-------	person on a tram, train or bus looking after tickets
malice-----------	evil intent or hatred
imminent-------	about to happen
knapsack-------	soldiers' or travellers' bag carried on the back
entangled-------	caught or mixed up in a tangle
adamant--------	determined and resolute
amorini---------	mythical artistic baby with wings
griffins----------	mythical creature with lion's body and eagle's head

INDEX

MULTIPLE-CHOICE

ENGLISH

Practice Test 8

Guidance for completing this Test.

1.   Read the passages carefully.

2.   Read the questions thoroughly.

3.   Read the answers carefully.

4.   Choose what you think is the correct answer carefully.

5.   Underline or circle the answer, immediately after the question.

6.   Transfer the LETTER **A,B,C,D,E** or **N** to the answer sheet.

7.   Make sure to mark the answer box like [—] not [╱].

8.   Check carefully that you have transferred your correct answer.

9 .   This test lasts for **50 minutes.**

PUPIL'S NAME _____

TOTAL MARK (Out of 60)	

Read this passage and answer the questions which follow. If there are any words you don't understand you may find them in the Glossary at the end of the test.

AUNT LIZZY'S DILEMMA

1.   Cathy's name was Cathy Kerr and she lived in Fern Avenue in the town of Durren. It wasn't a large town but was growing at a rapid pace. Her house was situated on the edge of the town; it was a large square building, white with green blinds and it

5.   had a porch at the front over which hung roses and clematis. Four tall poplar trees shaded the gravel path which ran down to the front gate. There was an orchard on one side of the house while on the other were piles of wood and a barn and an ice house.

        At the rear of the house was a kitchen garden sloping to the

10. south and filled with all the vegetables needed for a large family. Further back there was the pasture, providing grazing for four cows and through which ran a small stream and butternut trees growing in the corners. Two of the cattle were red while one was yellow with sharp horns tipped with tin and a lovely little

15. white one named Maisy.

        The Kerr family was composed of six children, two boys and four girls. Cathy was the oldest, just twelve years old while the youngest, Tim, was four. Their father was a doctor who was away from home all day and sometimes all night tending

20. to his sick patients. The family had lost their mother shortly after young Tim had been born. Cathy remembered her mother very well but the others had only descriptions of her given by their father to remind them of a sweet, gentle lady.

        The duties of the children's mother were taken over by the

25. father's sister Aunt Lizzy, who had come at the time when the younger children were told that their mother had gone on a long journey. They always kept hoping that she would return. Aunt Lizzy was a small woman, sharp-faced and thin, rather old-looking and very neat and particular about everything.

30.   She was anxious to be kind to the children but she had difficulty understanding them since they didn't behave as she had in her youth. She had been a gentle, tidy, frail child who loved to sit in the parlour, sewing long seams on various clothing items and being patted on the head by older people and being

35. informed that she was a good girl.

        Aunt Lizzy found that her charges were so different; Cathy tore her dress every day, hated sewing and didn't care a button

about being called 'good' while Claire and Eileen recoiled like restless ponies when anyone tried to pat their heads. It was
40. puzzling for Aunt Lizzy who found the children 'strange' and so little like the good boys and girls in her Sunday-school memories, who were the young people she liked best and understood most.

Her brother, Dr. Kerr, was another person who worried her. He wanted his children to be hardy and strong and
45. encouraged rough-play and climbing in spite of the bumps and torn clothing and cuts and bruises that resulted from such high jinks. The only occasion about which Aunt Lizzy had complete say was the half hour before breakfast when she made the rule that all the children would sit around her and learn a bible verse.

Answer the following questions. Look back over the passage. You should choose the _best_ answer and mark its letter on your answer sheet.

1. Who took over the mothering of the Kerr family ?

A. Dr. Kerr
C. Tim
E. the Mother's sister

B. Cathy
D. Dr. Kerr's sister

2. Who didn't like being patted on the head ?

A. Cathy and Tim
C. Eileen and Claire
D. Aunt Lizzy and Cathy

B. Dr. Kerr and Aunt Lizzy
D. Tim and Dr. Kerr

3. The outcome of Dr. Kerr's encouragement for his children to climb and play in a rough manner was

A. that Aunt Lizzy wouldn't look after the children.
B. that Dr. Kerr lost a lot of patients.
C. that there were complaints by neighbours.
D. that the children had to sit still for half an hour every day.
E. that the children suffered cuts, bruises and torn clothes.

4. What were growing in the corners of the pasture ?

A. red cows
C. roses
E. poplar trees

B. vegetables
D. butternut trees

2.

5.   The younger children had been told that their mother

A.   ...was in hospital being treated for an illness.
B.   ...had gone away on a long journey.
C.   ...had gone to the seaside.
D.   ...been sent away by Aunt Lizzy.
E.   ...died when giving birth to Tim.

6.   Aunt Lizzy had difficulty understanding the children

A.   ...when they didn't behave as she had in her young days.
B.   ...when they were sitting learning the bible verse.
C.   ...after they had come back from Sunday school.
D.   ...when their father told them to play as they liked.
E.   ...when they were riding their restless ponies.

7.   What relation was Aunt Lizzy to the children's real mother ?

A.   mother   B.   aunt
C.   sister   D.   sister-in-law
E.   mother-in-law

8.   What was distinctive about the porch of the Kerr house ?

A.   ...it was attached to the side of the house.
B.   ...it was overshadowed by poplar trees.
C.   ...clematis and roses drooped over it.
D.   ...it had a green framed door.
E.   ...it reached above the roof of the house.

9.   The family didn't see their father very often because

A.   ...he was away at sea a lot.
B.   ...he was a busy doctor.
C.   ...he trusted his sister to look after them.
D.   ...he was still very sad about his wife.
E.   ...he worked in a foreign country.

10.   The words that describe Aunt Lizzy as a child are

A.   frail and tidy   B.   sweet and gentle
C.   sharp-faced and thin   D.   rough and strange
E.   small and robust

3.

The following passage contains a number of mistakes. You have to find the mistakes. On each line there is either *one* mistake or *no* mistake. Find the group of words in which there is a mistake and mark the letter for it on your answer sheet. If there is no mistake, mark N.
First, look for the *spelling* mistakes.

11. At this | tyme she looked | at them with | pleased eyes for the
    A | B | C | D | N

12. the children | where all spick | and span with | nicely brushed
    A | B | C | D | N

13. coats and their | hair neatly | combed. But the | momant the
    A | B | C | D | N

14. bell rang to | signal the end | of the half-hour | Bibble session
    A | B | C | D | N

15. her comfort was | over. Fom that time | on they were | what she
    A | B | C | D | N

16. called "not fit | to be seen ". | The neighbours pitied | her very
    A | B | C | D | N

17. much. They | used to see the | countless items | of washing
    A | B | C | D | N

18. that were | hang out to dry | every Monday | morning and
    A | B | C | D | N

19. say to each | other what a load | of washing | thos children
    A | B | C | D | N

20. maid and | what a task it | must be for | Miss Kerr to keep
    A | B | C | D | N

them so nice.

Now look for *punctuation* mistakes.

21. But poor | Miss Kerr | didn t think | them nice at all.
    A | B | C | D | N

22. "Claire, go | upstairs and | wash your hands ! | eileen, pick
    A | B | C | D | N

4.

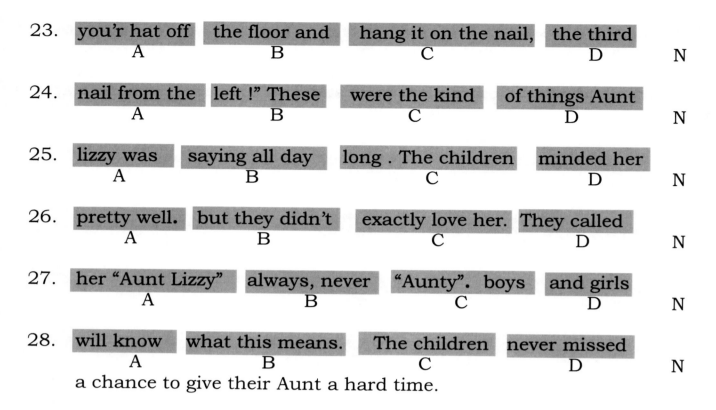

23. | you'r hat off | the floor and | hang it on the nail, | the third |
| :-: | :-: | :-: | :-: |
| A | B | C | D | N

24. | nail from the | left !" These | were the kind | of things Aunt |
| :-: | :-: | :-: | :-: |
| A | B | C | D | N

25. | lizzy was | saying all day | long . The children | minded her |
| :-: | :-: | :-: | :-: |
| A | B | C | D | N

26. | pretty well. | but they didn't | exactly love her. | They called |
| :-: | :-: | :-: | :-: |
| A | B | C | D | N

27. | her "Aunt Lizzy" | always, never | "Aunty". boys | and girls |
| :-: | :-: | :-: | :-: |
| A | B | C | D | N

28. | will know | what this means. | The children | never missed |
| :-: | :-: | :-: | :-: |
| A | B | C | D | N

a chance to give their Aunt a hard time.

Read this passage and answer the questions which follow. If there are any words you don't understand you may find them in the Glossary at the end of the test.

TOY TRAINS

1.   The earliest toy trains date from the 19th century and were often made of cast iron. Motorized units running on track soon followed, powered by a steam or clockwork engine. Some of these trains used clever methods to whistle and smoke.

5.   Toy trains were revolutionized when Marklin, a German firm that specialized in doll house accessories, sought to create an equivalent toy for boys where a constant revenue stream could be ensured by selling add-on accessories for years after the initial purchase. In addition to boxed sets containing a train and track,

10. Marklin offered extra track, rolling stock, and buildings sold separately, creating the predecessor to the modern model train layout featuring buildings and scenery in addition to an operating train.

      Electric trains followed, with the first appearing in 1897,

15. produced by the U.S. firm Carlisle & Finch. As electricity became more common in the early 20th century, electric trains gained popularity and as time went on, these electric trains grew in complexity, gaining lighting, the ability to change direction, to emit a whistling sound, to smoke, to remotely couple and

20. uncouple cars and even load and unload cargo. Toy trains from the first half of the 20th century were often made of lithographed tin; some later trains were made mostly of plastic.

5.

Prior to the 1950s, there was little distinction between toy trains and model railroads—model railroads were toys by
25. definition. Pull toys and wind-up trains were marketed towards children, while electric trains were marketed towards teenagers, particularly teenage boys. It was during the 1950s that the modern emphasis on realism in model railroading started to catch on.
A colorful EMD GP40-2 emblazoned with the Chessie System logo,
30. one of many wooden toy trains was offered by Whittle Shortline. Consumer interest in trains as toys waned in the late 1950s, but has experienced resurgence since the late 1990s due in large part to the popularity of Thomas the Tank Engine.
Today, S gauge and O gauge railroads are still considered toy
35. trains even by their supporters and are often accessorized with semi-scale model buildings by Plasticville or K-Line (who owns the rights to the Plasticville-like buildings produced by Marx from the 1950s to the 1970s). Ironically, however, due to their high cost, one is more likely to find an HO scale or N scale train set in a toy store
40. than an O scale set.
Many modern electric toy trains contain sophisticated electronics that emit digitized sound effects and allow the operator to safely and easily run multiple remote control trains on one loop of track.
45. Wooden toy trains are small toy trains that run on a wooden track system. The wooden tracks feature grooves to guide the wheels of the rolling stock. Wooden toy trains, tracks and scenery accessories are made mainly of wood. However, the wooden trains connect to each other using metal hooks or small magnets.
50. Some manufacturers also use plastic wheels mounted on metal axles for the rolling stock.

29. The first electric toy train was produced

A.   in the 19th century
C.   in the early 20th century
E.   in the 1970s

B.   in the year 1897
D.   in the 1950s

30. Carlisle and Finch were

A.   ...the first company to make wooden toy trains.
B.   ...the first German company to use plastic in trains.
C.   ...the first US company to make electric trains.
D.   ...the first German company to make electric trains.
E.   ...first US company to put modern electronics in toy trains.

31. The German company which revolutionized toy trains also specialised in

A. wooden toy trains.
B. board games.
C. toy farms.
D. accessories for dolls' houses.
E. plastic to trains.

32. The toy trains which were made from lithographed tin were manufactured

A. ...in the first half of the 20th century.
B. ...in the second half of the 20th century.
C. ...in the 19th century.
D. ...from the 1950s to 1970s.
E. ...in 1897.

33. The other accessories used in the making of wooden toy trains are

A. ...plastic tracks and rolling stock.
B. ...metal axles and plastic wheels.
C. ...electronic whistling and digital sound.
D. ...lighting and smoke.
E. ...extra track and station buildings.

34. The company which owns the rights to the semi-scale Plasticville model buildings is

A. Marx
B. Marklin
C. Carlisle and Finch
D. Chessie System
E. K-line

35. The innovation which the German manufacturer, Marklin, introduced was

A. ...a range of different coloured trains and rolling stock.
B. ...electronics to power digitised sound effects and lighting.
C. ...producing add-on accessories for sale after the first purchase.
D. ...the introduction of steam or clockwise engines.
E. ...the mechanisms for automatically changing signals and lines.

SET 3 Blank Answer Sheets
ENGLISH Test 7
ENGLISH Test 8
ENGLISH Test 9

Instructions for completing the Answer Sheet.

1. You must concentrate fully when recording your answers.

    --take your time when recording your answers--

    --make sure you have the correct answer number--

    --make sure you select the correct letter, A, B, C, D, E or N--

2. Use a pencil to mark your answer, A, B, C, D, E or N.

3. Mark your answer like this---- (~~A~~) (B) (C) (D) (E) (N)

    (A) (B) (~~C~~) (D) (E) (N)

    (A) (B) (C) (D) (E) (~~N~~)

    ALWAYS USE A HORIZONTAL (—) LINE

4. DO NOT MARK like this-- (A) (B) (C) (Ɗ) (E) (N)

    (A) (B) (✕) (D) (E) (N)

    (A) (✗) (C) (D) (E) (N)

    (A) (B) (C) (D) (✗) (N)

5. If you make a mistake, rub out the line, select the correct answer and draw a line through the correct letter.

6. It might be an idea to answer 5 questions at a time and then record these 5 answers all at the same time.

7. When reading the questions you record the answers on the question paper. When you have completed 5 questions on the question paper you then record these on the Answer sheet. Proceed to record another 5 questions.

ANSWER SHEETS   English Test 7

Please mark the boxes like (—), not like (/). Rub out mistakes thoroughly.

Pages 2 & 3.

1	(A) (B) (C) (D) (E)	6	(A) (B) (C) (D) (E)
2	(A) (B) (C) (D) (E)	7	(A) (B) (C) (D) (E)
3	(A) (B) (C) (D) (E)	8	(A) (B) (C) (D) (E)
4	(A) (B) (C) (D) (E)	9	(A) (B) (C) (D) (E)
5	(A) (B) (C) (D) (E)	10	(A) (B) (C) (D) (E)

Pages 4

Spelling

11	(A) (B) (C) (D) (N)	16	(A) (B) (C) (D) (N)
12	(A) (B) (C) (D) (N)	17	(A) (B) (C) (D) (N)
13	(A) (B) (C) (D) (N)	18	(A) (B) (C) (D) (N)
14	(A) (B) (C) (D) (N)	19	(A) (B) (C) (D) (N)
15	(A) (B) (C) (D) (N)	20	(A) (B) (C) (D) (N)

Page 4 & 5.

Punctuation

21	(A) (B) (C) (D) (N)	25	(A) (B) (C) (D) (N)
22	(A) (B) (C) (D) (N)	26	(A) (B) (C) (D) (N)
23	(A) (B) (C) (D) (N)	27	(A) (B) (C) (D) (N)
24	(A) (B) (C) (D) (N)	28	(A) (B) (C) (D) (N)

Pages 6, 7 & 8.

29	(A) (B) (C) (D) (E)	36	(A) (B) (C) (D) (E)
30	(A) (B) (C) (D) (E)	37	(A) (B) (C) (D) (E)
31	(A) (B) (C) (D) (E)	38	(A) (B) (C) (D) (E)
32	(A) (B) (C) (D) (E)	39	(A) (B) (C) (D) (E)
33	(A) (B) (C) (D) (E)	40	(A) (B) (C) (D) (E)
34	(A) (B) (C) (D) (E)	41	(A) (B) (C) (D) (E)
35	(A) (B) (C) (D) (E)	42	(A) (B) (C) (D) (E)

Pages 9, 10 & 11.

43	(A) (B) (C) (D) (E)	49	(A) (B) (C) (D) (E)
44	(A) (B) (C) (D) (E)	50	(A) (B) (C) (D) (E)
45	(A) (B) (C) (D) (E)	51	(A) (B) (C) (D) (E)
46	(A) (B) (C) (D) (E)	52	(A) (B) (C) (D) (E)
47	(A) (B) (C) (D) (E)	53	(A) (B) (C) (D) (E)
48	(A) (B) (C) (D) (E)	54	(A) (B) (C) (D) (E)
		55	(A) (B) (C) (D) (E)

Pages 12 & 13

General Section

56	(a) (A) (B) (C) (D)	58	(b) (A) (B) (C) (D)
	(b) (A) (B) (C) (D)	59	(a) (A) (B) (C) (D)
57	(a) (A) (B) (C) (D)		(b) (A) (B) (C) (D)
	(b) (A) (B) (C) (D)	60	(a) (A) (B) (C) (D)
58	(a) (A) (B) (C) (D)		(b) (A) (B) (C) (D)

Multiple Choice English
Test 7 Answer Key.

THE BAKING PROCESS
1. B
2. C
3. D
4. B
5. B
6. A
7. D
8. D
9. C
10. A

Spelling
11. D--nearest
12. C--picnic
13. C--appalled
14. N
15. D--hazard
16. A--beach
17. B--discarded
18. C--footwear
19. B--rubbish
20. C--relieve

Punctuation
21. C--question mark needed
22. B--apostrophe needed
23. D--no question mark
24. D--its
25. C--contents
26. B--no full stop
27. N
28. B--no full stop

FAMILY OF NINE
29. C
30. E
31. C
32. A
33. D
34. E
35. B
36. B
37. D
38. C
39. C
40. A
41. D
42. D

FLORENCE FROM A WINDOW
43. C
44. B
45. C
46. A
47. E
48. D
49. B
50. B
51. C
52. A
53. E
54. C
55. D

General Section

	(a)		(b).	
56.	(a)	D	(b).	D
57.	(a)	C	(b).	D
58.	(a)	A	(b).	B
59.	(a)	D	(b).	B
60.	(a)	C	(b).	D

Multiple Choice English
Test 8 Answer Key.

AUNT LIZZY'S DILEMMA

1. D
2. C
3. E
4. D
5. B
6. A
7. D
8. C
9. B
10. A

Spelling

11. B--time
12. B--were
13. D--moment
14. D--Bible
15. B--from
16. C--neighbours
17. N
18. B--hung
19. D--those
20. A--made

Punctuation

21. C--apostrophe missing
22. D--Eileen
23. A--no apostrophe
24. N
25. A--Lizzy
26. A--no full stop
27. C--no full stop
28. N

TOY TRAINS

29. B
30. C
31. D
32. A
33. B
34. E
35. C
36. D
37. C
38. A
39. C
40. A
41. D
42. B

GRADGRIND FAMILY

43. C
44. E
45. E
46. C
47. D
48. A
49. C
50. B
51. C
52. D
53. A
54. B
55. D

General Section

56.	(a)	B	(b).	A
57.	(a)	D	(b).	A
58.	(a)	B	(b).	B
59.	(a)	C	(b).	B
60.	(a)	B	(b).	D

Multiple Choice English
Test 9 Answer Key.

THE LIFE OF BLYTON

1. E
2. C
3. B
4. A
5. B
6. B
7. E
8. C
9. A
10. C

Spelling

11. D--crisis
12. B--decided
13. C--because
14. D--services
15. N
16. D--School
17. B--marriage
18. N
19. C--began
20. A--which

Punctuation

21. N
22. A--no exclamation mark
23. C--no apostrophe
24. B--no question mark
25. A--no comma
26. N
27. C--doctor's
28. B--no speech marks

LAST of the PHAIRS

29. A
30. D
31. B
32. D
33. E
34. B
35. C
36. B
37. D
38. D
39. C
40. E
41. B
42. D

KINGS of the JUNGLE

43. B
44. C
45. E
46. C
47. E
48. D
49. A
50. D
51. D
52. B
53. B
54. D
55. E

General section

56.	(a) C	(b).	B
57.	(a) B	(b).	B
58.	(a) C	(b).	B
59.	(a) A	(b).	D
60.	(a) C	(b).	B

English Test 8

Please mark the boxes like (—), not like (╱). Rub out mistakes thoroughly.

Pages 2 & 3.

1 (A)(B)(C)(D)(E)		6 (A)(B)(C)(D)(E)
2 (A)(B)(C)(D)(E)		7 (A)(B)(C)(D)(E)
3 (A)(B)(C)(D)(E)		8 (A)(B)(C)(D)(E)
4 (A)(B)(C)(D)(E)		9 (A)(B)(C)(D)(E)
5 (A)(B)(C)(D)(E)		10 (A)(B)(C)(D)(E)

Pages 4
Spelling

11 (A)(B)(C)(D)(N)	16 (A)(B)(C)(D)(N)
12 (A)(B)(C)(D)(N)	17 (A)(B)(C)(D)(N)
13 (A)(B)(C)(D)(N)	18 (A)(B)(C)(D)(N)
14 (A)(B)(C)(D)(N)	19 (A)(B)(C)(D)(N)
15 (A)(B)(C)(D)(N)	20 (A)(B)(C)(D)(N)

Page 4 & 5
Punctuation

21 (A)(B)(C)(D)(N)	25 (A)(B)(C)(D)(N)
22 (A)(B)(C)(D)(N)	26 (A)(B)(C)(D)(N)
23 (A)(B)(C)(D)(N)	27 (A)(B)(C)(D)(N)
24 (A)(B)(C)(D)(N)	28 (A)(B)(C)(D)(N)

Pages 6, 7 & 8.

29 (A)(B)(C)(D)(E)	36 (A)(B)(C)(D)(E)
30 (A)(B)(C)(D)(E)	37 (A)(B)(C)(D)(E)
31 (A)(B)(C)(D)(E)	38 (A)(B)(C)(D)(E)
32 (A)(B)(C)(D)(E)	39 (A)(B)(C)(D)(E)
33 (A)(B)(C)(D)(E)	40 (A)(B)(C)(D)(E)
34 (A)(B)(C)(D)(E)	41 (A)(B)(C)(D)(E)
35 (A)(B)(C)(D)(E)	42 (A)(B)(C)(D)(E)

Pages 10, 11 & 12.

43 (A)(B)(C)(D)(E)	49 (A)(B)(C)(D)(E)
44 (A)(B)(C)(D)(E)	50 (A)(B)(C)(D)(E)
45 (A)(B)(C)(D)(E)	51 (A)(B)(C)(D)(E)
46 (A)(B)(C)(D)(E)	52 (A)(B)(C)(D)(E)
47 (A)(B)(C)(D)(E)	53 (A)(B)(C)(D)(E)
48 (A)(B)(C)(D)(E)	54 (A)(B)(C)(D)(E)
	55 (A)(B)(C)(D)(E)

Pages 12 & 13
General Section

56 (a) (A)(B)(C)(D)	58 (b) (A)(B)(C)(D)
(b) (A)(B)(C)(D)	59 (a) (A)(B)(C)(D)
57 (a) (A)(B)(C)(D)	(b) (A)(B)(C)(D)
(b) (A)(B)(C)(D)	60 (a) (A)(B)(C)(D)
58 (a) (A)(B)(C)(D)	(b) (A)(B)(C)(D)

English Test 9

Please mark the boxes like (——), not like (/). Rub out mistakes thoroughly.

Pages 2 & 3.

1 (A)(B)(C)(D)(E)		6 (A)(B)(C)(D)(E)
2 (A)(B)(C)(D)(E)		7 (A)(B)(C)(D)(E)
3 (A)(B)(C)(D)(E)		8 (A)(B)(C)(D)(E)
4 (A)(B)(C)(D)(E)		9 (A)(B)(C)(D)(E)
5 (A)(B)(C)(D)(E)		10 (A)(B)(C)(D)(E)

Pages 4

Spelling

11 (A)(B)(C)(D)(N)	16 (A)(B)(C)(D)(N)
12 (A)(B)(C)(D)(N)	17 (A)(B)(C)(D)(N)
13 (A)(B)(C)(D)(N)	18 (A)(B)(C)(D)(N)
14 (A)(B)(C)(D)(N)	19 (A)(B)(C)(D)(N)
15 (A)(B)(C)(D)(N)	20 (A)(B)(C)(D)(N)

Page 4 & 5

Punctuation

21 (A)(B)(C)(D)(N)	25 (A)(B)(C)(D)(N)
22 (A)(B)(C)(D)(N)	26 (A)(B)(C)(D)(N)
23 (A)(B)(C)(D)(N)	27 (A)(B)(C)(D)(N)
24 (A)(B)(C)(D)(N)	28 (A)(B)(C)(D)(N)

Pages 6, 7 & 8.

29 (A)(B)(C)(D)(E)	36 (A)(B)(C)(D)(E)
30 (A)(B)(C)(D)(E)	37 (A)(B)(C)(D)(E)
31 (A)(B)(C)(D)(E)	38 (A)(B)(C)(D)(E)
32 (A)(B)(C)(D)(E)	39 (A)(B)(C)(D)(E)
33 (A)(B)(C)(D)(E)	40 (A)(B)(C)(D)(E)
34 (A)(B)(C)(D)(E)	41 (A)(B)(C)(D)(E)
35 (A)(B)(C)(D)(E)	42 (A)(B)(C)(D)(E)

Pages 10, 11 & 12.

43 (A)(B)(C)(D)(E)	49 (A)(B)(C)(D)(E)
44 (A)(B)(C)(D)(E)	50 (A)(B)(C)(D)(E)
45 (A)(B)(C)(D)(E)	51 (A)(B)(C)(D)(E)
46 (A)(B)(C)(D)(E)	52 (A)(B)(C)(D)(E)
47 (A)(B)(C)(D)(E)	53 (A)(B)(C)(D)(E)
48 (A)(B)(C)(D)(E)	54 (A)(B)(C)(D)(E)
	55 (A)(B)(C)(D)(E)

Pages 12 & 13

General Section

56 (a) (A)(B)(C)(D)	58 (b) (A)(B)(C)(D)
(b) (A)(B)(C)(D)	59 (a) (A)(B)(C)(D)
57 (a) (A)(B)(C)(D)	(b) (A)(B)(C)(D)
(b) (A)(B)(C)(D)	60 (a) (A)(B)(C)(D)
58 (a) (A)(B)(C)(D)	(b) (A)(B)(C)(D)

36. A resurgence in toy trains in the 1990s happened because of

A.   ...the Chessie System logo.   B.   ...the EMD GP40-2.
C.   ...the HO and N scale trains.   D.   ...Thomas the Tank Engine.
E.   ...consumer interest.

37. The material from which the earliest toy trains were made was

A.   wood   B.   plastic   C.   cast iron
D.   stainless steel   E.   lithographed tin

38. Which of the following is a feature of the modern electric
    toy trains (in second-last paragraph)?

A.   ...multiple remote control trains.   B.   ...plastic wheels.
C.   ...S and O gauge railways.   D.   ...lithographed tin.
E.   ...remotely operated engines.

39. The best meaning for the phrase "has experienced resurgence" is

A.   ...caused a definite decline.   B.   ...has created a decrease.
C.   ...has resulted in a revival.   D.   ...has been a reorganisation.
E.   ...has resulted in a fall.

40. The meaning of the word "predecessor" in line 11 is

A.   forerunner   B.   forefinger
C.   family   D.   company
E.   descendant

41. There are FIVE nouns in

A.   line 24   B.   line 50   C.   line 18
D.   line 47   E.   line 25

42. The words add-on in line 8, semi-scale in line 36 and
    Plastiville-like are

A.   proper nouns   B.   hyphenated words
C.   compound words   D.   collective nouns
E.   proper adjectives

8.

Read this passage and answer the questions which follow. If there are any words you don't understand you may find them in the Glossary at the end of the test.

GRADGRIND FAMILY

1.   Mr. Gradgrind, whose voice is "dictatorial", opens the novel by stating "Now, what I want is facts" at his school in Coketown. He is a man of "facts and calculations." He interrogates one of his pupils, Sissy, whose father is involved
5.   with the circus.

       Since her father rides and tends to horses, Gradgrind offers Sissy the definition of "veterinary surgeon." She is rebuffed for not being able to define a horse factually; her classmate Bitzer does, however, provide a more zoological profile description and
10. factual definition. She does not learn easily, and is censured for suggesting that she would carpet a floor with pictures of flowers.

       Louisa and Tom, two of Mr. Gradgrind's children, pay a visit after school to the touring circus run by Mr. Sleary, only to find their father, who is angry and annoyed by their trip
15. since he believes the circus to be the bastion of fancy and conceit. Being led by their father, Louisa and Tom trudge off in a despondent mood. Mr. Gradgrind has three younger children.

       Gradgrind apprehends Louisa and Tom, his two eldest children, at the circus. Josiah Bounderby, "a man perfectly devoid
20. of sentiment", is revealed as being Gradgrind's boss. Bounderby is a manufacturer and millowner, who is prosperous as a result of his enterprise and capital. Bounderby is what one might call a "self-made man" who has risen from the gutter. He is not averse to giving dramatic summaries of his childhood, which terrify Mr.
25. Gradgrind's weak wife who is often rendered unfeeling by these horrific stories. He is described in a bitter manner as being "the Bully of Humility."

       Mr. Gradgrind and Bounderby visit the public-house where Sissy resides to inform her that she cannot attend the school
30. anymore due to the risk of her ideas spreading in the class. Sissy meets the two collaborators, informing them her father has abandoned her not out of malice, but out of desire for Sissy to lead a better life without him. This was the reasoning behind him enlisting her at Gradgrind's school and Gradgrind is outraged at
35. this claim.

       At this point members of the circus appear, led by their manager Mr. Sleary. Mr. Gradgrind gives Sissy a choice: either to return to the circus and forfeit her education, or to continue her education and never to return to the circus. Sleary and Gradgrind

40.	both have their say on the matter, and at the behest of Josephine Sleary, Sissy decides to leave the circus and bid all the close friends she had formed farewell.

	Back at the Gradgrind house, Tom and Louisa sit down and discuss their feelings, however repressing they seem to be. Tom,
45.	already at this present stage of education finds himself in a state of dissatisfaction, and Louisa also expresses her discontent at her childhood while staring into the fire. Louisa's ability to wonder, however, has not been entirely extinguished by her rigorous education based in fact.
50.	We are introduced to the workers at the mills, known as the "Hands". Amongst them is a man named Stephen Blackpool or "Old Stephen" who has led a toilsome life. He is described as a "man of perfect integrity". He has ended his day's work, and his close companion Rachael is about somewhere. He eventually
55.	meets up with her, and they walk home discussing their day.

43.	The main character in the passage, Mr. Gradgrind, works

A.	...in the circus			B.	...as a manager
C.	...as a teacher			D.	...as a horse trainer
E.	...in a mill

44.	How many children has Mr. Gradgrind ?

A.	one		B.	two		C.	three
D.	four		E.	five

45.	Who persuaded Sissy to leave the circus ?

A.	Mr. Gradgrind		B.	Mr. Bounderby		C.	Mr. Sleary
D.	Tom and Louisa		E.	Josephine Sleary

46.	How are the workers at the mills described ?

A.	repressed		B.	rigorous		C.	hands
D.	collaborators		E.	affluent

47.	Who is described as **"the Bully of Humility"** ?

A.	Mr. Gradgrind			B.	Josephine Sleary
C.	Stephen Blackpool		D.	Mr. Bounderby
E.	Mr. Sleary

48. Who walked home together discussing their day ?

A. Rachael and Old Stephen.
B. Tom and Louisa.
C. Mr. Bounderby and Mr. Gradgrind.
D. Josephine and Mr. Sleary.
E. Stephen Blackpool and Sissy.

49. What is the choice that is given to Sissy ?

A. ...to stay at school and join the circus.
B. ...to join the circus and leave home.
C. ...to stay at school and leave the circus.
D. ...to work in the mill and join the circus.
E. ...to join the circus and work in the zoo.

50. The TWO phrases which best describe Joshua Bounderby are

A. ...man of integrity and generous.
B. ...self-made and without sentiment.
C. ...factual and humble.
D. ...manufacturer and teacher.
E. ...circus owner and bully.

51. The person described as one of **"facts and calculations"** is

A. Stephen Blackpool   B. Josephine Sleary
C. Mr. Gradgrind   D. Josiah Bounderby
E. Mr. Sleary

52. A zoological description of a horse was given by

A. Thomas   B. Sissy   C. Louisa
D. Bitzer   E. Mr. Gradgrind

53. The word which means the same as **toilsome** is

A. hardworking   B. satisfactory   C. sweating
D. industrial   E. harsh

54. Which TWO words in the second paragraph have the same meaning as **explanation or meaning** ?

A. factually / factual
B. definition / description
C. censured / picture
D. learn / define
E. carpet / picture

55. The adverb in **line 48** is

A. however
B. rigorous
C. been
D. entirely
E. extinguished

General Section

To answer these questions, you may have to think about the passages you have read. Look back at these if you need to. Look also at the Index and Glossary.

56. (a) Poetry could be described as

A. ...ordinary writing using sentences and paragraphs.
B. ...imaginative writing in rhythmic lines.
C. ...literary works in imaginative fashion.
D. ...long fictitious story in book form.

(b). The Title in the INDEX which has an apostrophe is

A. AUNT LIZZY'S DILEMMA
B. General Section
C. TOY TRAINS
D. GRADGRIND FAMILY

57. (a) The words which are nouns in the GLOSSARY are

A. remotely / dictatorial
B. devoid / grazing
C. revolutionized / repressed
D. revenue / collaborators

(b). The pair of words which have opposite meanings are

A. friend / foe
B. liberty / freedom
C. miserable / dejected
D. permanent / lasting

58. (a) In which of the following sentence is there a grammatical error ?

A. The teacher chose Jim and me to be the captains.
B. Harry and me went to the swimming pool.
C. Granny called Mary and gave her a bag of sweets.
D. My father sent my sister and me to the shop.

(b). Which word in the Glossary is something that some animals do ?

A. digitized   B. grazing
C. repressing   D. revolutionized

59. (a) Which pair of words in the GLOSSARY are associated with people ?

A. grazing and accessories   B. devoid and remotely
C. mothering and collaborators   D. bastion and emit

(b). The words in the INDEX section that are associated with manufacturing companies are

A. Durren and Fern Avenue   B. Carlisle and Finch
C. Stephen Blackpool   D. Thomas the Tank Engine

Choose the correct adverb from the list in each sentence.

60. (a) The gymnasium is situated **definitely** **conveniently**
                                        A   B
   squarely **finely** to the school.
      C   D

(b). The rainswept road was **dimly** **happily** **feebly** **brilliantly**
                                   A   B   C   D
lit up by the lorry's headlights.

13.

GLOSSARY

clematis------- climbing garden plant
tending-------- taking care of
grazing-------- eating grass usually by animals
frail----------- fragile, weak
mothering----- acting as a mother, bringing up a family
revolutionized-change considerably
accessories---- additional relation parts
revenue------- income of a country usually raised by taxes
complexity---- elaborate involving many aspects
emit----------- give out either heat or light
remotely------ isolated, distant
lithographed-- printed from metal or stone templates
resurgence---- revival, resumption, re-emergence
digitized------ information displayed in numbers
dictatorial----- imposing one's will on people or groups
disconcerted-- upsetting
bastion-------- strong defence against enemy or ideas
despondent--- unhappy, depressed, downhearted
devoid-------- lacking, deficient, free from
collaborators-- co-worker, associate, colleague
behest--------- an order or a strong request
repressing---- kept feelings in check

INDEX

MULTIPLE-CHOICE
ENGLISH
Practice Test 9

Guidance for completing this Test.

1. Read the passages carefully.

2. Read the questions thoroughly.

3. Read the answers carefully.

4. Choose what you think is the correct answer carefully.

5. Underline or circle the answer, immediately after the question.

6. Transfer the LETTER **A,B,C,D,E** or **N** to the answer sheet.

7. Make sure to mark the answer box like [—] not [╱].

8. Check carefully that you have transferred your correct answer.

9. This test lasts for **50 minutes**.

PUPIL'S NAME _____

TOTAL MARK (Out of 60)	

**Read this passage and answer the questions which follow.
If there are any words you don't understand you may find
them in the Glossary at the end of the test.**

THE LIFE OF BLYTON

1.   Enid Mary Blyton (11 August 1897 – 28 November 1968)
was a British children's writer known as both Enid Blyton and
Mary Pollock. She was one of the most successful children's
storytellers of the twentieth century. Once described as a "one-
5.   woman fiction machine", she is noted for numerous series of
books based on recurring characters and designed for different
age groups.
        Her books have enjoyed popular success in many parts of the
world, and have sold over 400 million copies. Blyton is the sixth
10. most translated author worldwide: she is behind Lenin and almost
equal to Shakespeare.
        One of her most widely known characters is Noddy, intended
for early years readers. However, her main forte is the young
readers' novels, where children ride out their own adventures with
15. minimal adult help. In this genre, particularly popular series
include the Famous Five (consisting of 21 novels, 1942–1963, based
on four children and their dog), the Five Find-Outers and Dog, (15
novels, 1943–1961, where five children regularly outwit the local
police) as well as the Secret Seven (15 novels, 1949–1963,
20. a society of seven children who solve various mysteries).
        Her work involves children's adventure stories, and fantasy,
sometimes involving magic. Her books were and still are
enormously popular in Britain, Malta, India, Pakistan, New
Zealand, Sri Lanka, Singapore, and Australia; and as translations
25. in the former Yugoslavia, Japan, and across most of the globe. Her
work has been translated into nearly 90 languages.
Blyton was born on 11 August 1897 at 354 Lordship Lane,
East Dulwich, London, the eldest child of Thomas Carey Blyton
(1870–1920), a salesman of cutlery, and his wife, Theresa Mary,
30. née Harrison (1874–1950). There were two younger brothers, Hanly
(b. 1899), and Carey (b. 1902), who were born after the family had
moved to the nearby suburb of Beckenham. From 1907 to 1915,
Blyton was educated at St. Christopher's School in Beckenham,
where she excelled at her endeavours, leaving as head girl. She
35. enjoyed all activities, along with the academic work,
but not Maths.
        Blyton was a talented pianist, but gave up her musical
studies when she trained as a teacher at Ipswich High School.

40. She taught for five years at Bickley, Surbiton and Chessington, writing in her spare time. Her first book, Child Whispers, a collection of poems, was published in 1922.

On 28 August 1924 Blyton married Major Hugh Alexander Pollock DS (1888–1971), editor of the book department in the publishing firm of George Newnes, which published two of her
45. books that year. The couple moved to Buckinghamshire. Eventually they moved to a house in Beaconsfield, named Green Hedges by Blyton's readers following a competition in Sunny Stories. They had two children: Gillian Mary Baverstock (15 July 1931 – 24 June 2007) and Imogen Mary Smallwood
50. (born 27 October 1935).

Answer the following questions. Look back over the passage. You should choose the _best_ answer and mark its letter on your answer sheet.

1. How much **older** was Enid Blyton than her brother Carey ?

A. 1 year   B. 2 years   C. 3 years
D. 4 years   E. 5 years

2. Enid Blyton lived for

A. 67 years   B. 69 years   C. 71 years
D. 73 years   E. 75 years

3. Enid Blyton's father was a

A. teacher   B. cutlery salesman
C. bookseller   D. pianist
E. publisher

4. How many novels about **The Secret Seven** did Enid Blyton write ?

A. 15 novels   B. 21 novels   C. 17 novels
D. 2 novels   E. 25 novels

5. The topics about which Enid Blyton wrote were

A. animals and school   B. adventure and fantasy
C. dogs and rural life   D. mystery and city life
E. teachers and pupils

2.

6. The names of Blyton's two brothers were

A. Thomas and Carey
B. Hanly and Carey
C. Hugh and Hanley
D. Hanley and Thomas
E. Carey and Harrison

7. The name of Enid Blyton's first book, a collection of poems, was

A. Noddy   B. Famous Five   C. Secret Seven
D. Green Hedges   E. Child Whispers

8. When did Enid Blyton give up her musical Studies ?

A. ...when she married.
B. ...when she wrote her first novel.
C. ...when she trained as a teacher.
D. ...when she and her husband moved house.
E. ...when she left St. Christopher's School.

9. The description of Enid Blyton used in the passage is

A. ...one-woman fiction machine.
B. ...most widely known character.
C. ...the most translated author worldwide.
D. ...better writer than Shakespeare.
E. ...enormously popular author.

10. How did Enid Blyton's family house in Beaconsfield get its name, **Green Hedges** ?

A. ...it was named by her two children.
B. ...it was called after the house in which she was born.
C. ...it was named by the readers of her book, Sunny Stories.
D. ...it was named by her publisher.
E. ...it was named by her husband, Major Pollock.

The following passage contains a number of mistakes. You have to find the mistakes. On each line there is either _one_ mistake or _no_ mistake. Find the group of words in which there is a mistake and mark the letter for it on your answer sheet. If there is no mistake, mark N.

First, look for the _spelling_ mistakes.

11. In the / mid-1930s / Blyton experienced / a spiritual crises,
    A   B   C   D   N

12. but she / desided against / converting to / Roman Catholicism
    A   B   C   D   N

13. from the Church / of England / becasue she had / felt it was "too
    A   B   C   D   N

14. restricting". Although / she rarely / attended church / servises,
    A   B   C   D   N

15. she saw that / her two daughters / were baptised / into the
    A   B   C   D   N

16. Anglican faith / and went / to the local / Sunday Scool.
    A   B   C   D   N

17. By 1939 her / mariage to Pollock / was in difficulties, / and in
    A   B   C   D   N

18. 1941 she met / Kenneth Fraser / Darrell-Waters / (1892–1967),
    A   B   C   D   N

19. a London / surgeon, with / whom she begin / a friendship
    A   B   C   D   N

20. witch quickly / developed into / something deeper. / After each
    A   B   C   D   N

Now look for _punctuation_ mistakes.

21. had divorced, / they married / at the City / of Westminster
    A   B   C   D   N

22. registry office ! / on 20 October / 1943, and / she subsequently
    A   B   C   D

N   4.

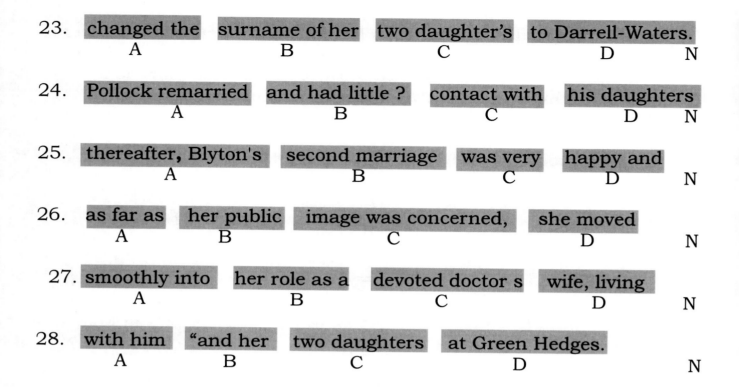

23. changed the | surname of her | two daughter's | to Darrell-Waters.
     A   B   C   D   N

24. Pollock remarried | and had little ? | contact with | his daughters
     A   B   C   D   N

25. thereafter, Blyton's | second marriage | was very | happy and
     A   B   C   D   N

26. as far as | her public | image was concerned, | she moved
     A   B   C   D   N

27. smoothly into | her role as a | devoted doctor s | wife, living
     A   B   C   D   N

28. with him | "and her | two daughters | at Green Hedges.
     A   B   C   D   N

Read this passage and answer the questions which follow. If there are any words you don't understand you may find them in the Glossary at the end of the test.

LAST OF THE PHAIRS

1. In the cottage at Pharaoh, Miss Leonis was reading by the bright light of a resiny fire. On a small table by her side lay a bible, closed. She was not certain that consulting it had caused her to make her decision to open Quentin Phair's
5. letters and journals, unread for so many generations, instead of waiting to leave them for Simon.

But ever since Mrs. O'Keefe had dropped her at Pharaoh, after an exhausting and stimulating afternoon, she had been restless and unable to settle down. Her sense of smell kept
10. telling her that something was wrong, but not what that something was, except that it had to do with Simon, who was miles away at sea in a small freighter heading into the Caribbean.

Had she been right to accept Forsyth Phair's invitation to take his young cousin to Caracas with him ? It would be a
15. journey of less than two weeks; they would be returning by plane after leaving the portrait in Caracas. Surely this was the opportunity for Simon which should not be turned down ?

Something is wrong, something is wrong, an inner voice continued to nag--Simon is in danger.

20.   Had her concern over Simon's future dulled her sense of
smell over Forsyth? Had he come with documents tracing his
descent from one of her great-uncles who had moved out west
after the war? She knew that this shared ancestor had undoubtedly
played politics with the carpetbaggers, but Forsyth Phair was
25. not to be blamed for that after all. Perhaps it was old-fashioned
prejudice which made her hold this against him.
      In any event, Forsyth was a Phair; his nose and chin told her
that, the high-bridged, hawk-like nose, though Forsyth's eyes
crowded close together, unlike the wide-spaced Phair eyes.
30. But he had the strong chin softened by an unexpected dimple which
usually turned into a formidable cleft by middle age.
      In Forsyth the cleft was almost a scar. Yes, he was a Phair,
and hanky-panky with those who wanted to get rich on the
troubles of the South was hardly to be blamed on him. His talk
35. of his life in Caracas sounded serious and surely it was
commendable that he wanted to return the portrait to his
adopted country rather than to keep it himself ? And then,
Forsyth was the last of the Phairs. Simon was a Renier. The male
line of Phairs had been prone to accident and sudden death.
40.   Pride of name, she thought wryly,--Is that part of it ?
Pride. Pride was always her downfall. When Simon's mother died she
had concealed the fact of her poverty from the Renier
relatives. They had wanted the boy to come to them, to his father's
people. She had to battle to keep him and she respected the
45. Reniers for letting Simon, in the end, make the choice. They
would be ready to take him to their hearts when she died. They
would see to it that he was properly educated, that he went to
medical school. If she had asked them for money they would have
given it to her. If she had asked them to buy the portrait they
50. would have bought it--but then she might have lost Simon.

29.   How were Forsyth Phair and his young cousin to return
from their visit to Caracas ?

A.   ...by plane.
C.   ...by boat.
E.   ...on horseback.

B.   ...by train.
D.   ...in a car.

30.   Miss Leonis was able to read in the cottage in Pharaoh using

A.   ...the light on the desk.
C.   ...the light from the moon.
E.   ...the light from the sun.

B.   ...the daylight.
D.   ...the light from a fire.

31. What kept telling Miss Leonis that **"something was wrong"** ?

A. ...the messages she was getting from Simon.
B. ...her sense of smell.
C. ...her decision to open the letters.
D. ...Mrs. O'Keefe had informed her.
E. ...a call from Forsyth Phair.

32. Who moved out **west** after the war ?

A. Forsyth Phair   B. Miss Leonis
C. Simon   D. Miss Leonis' great-uncle.
E. Mrs. O'Keefe.

33. Forsyth's nose is described as

A. ...a cleft like a scar.   B. ...wide-spaced
C. ...crowded close together.   D. ...strong but softened.
E. ...hawk-like.

34. The Reniers made sure that Simon would be

A. ...brought up by them after his father died.
B. ...educated properly and sent to medical school.
C. ...given all the money he needed.
D. ...saved from accident and death.
E. ...sent to Pharaoh after his mother died.

35. Miss Leonis' great-uncle had played politics with

A. ...his descendants.   B. ...people from the west.
C. ...the carpetbaggers.   D. ...members of his family.
E. ...the people of Pharaoh.

36. What turned into a cleft by middle age ?

A. ...the strong chin.   B. ...a dimple.
C. ...the high-bridged nose   D. ...wide-spaced eyes.
E. ...pointed ears.

37. Who is described as the **"last of the Phairs"** ?

A. Miss Leonis   B. Simon
C. Mrs. O'Keefe   D. Forsyth
E. Renier

38. How long would Forsyth's journey to Caracas last ?

A. ...less than a week.   B. ...less than a day.
C. ...less than a month.   D. ...less than two weeks.
E. ...less than a year.

39. The nouns in **line 21** are

A. smell / his   B. Forsyth / tracing
C. documents / Forsyth   D. come / had
E. he / his

40. The word **afternoon** in **line 8** and the word **downfall** in **line 41** are

A. proper nouns.   B. hyphenated words.
C. proper adjectives.   D. collective nouns.
E. compound words.

41. The best meaning for the phrase **"had been prone to accident"** in **line 39** is

A. ...caused an accident by lying down.
B. ...liable to be involved with misfortune.
C. ...had never been involved in a mishap.
D. ...disaster had always been avoided.
E. ...accidents happen to someone else.

42. The word in the second paragraph which means the same as **"exciting"** is

A. exhausting   B. restless
C. unable   D. stimulating
E. heading

Read this passage and answer the questions which follow. If there are any words you don't understand you may find them in the Glossary at the end of the test.

KINGS of the JUNGLE

1.   Lions are a major symbol of wild Africa. They have been worshipped and admired for their strength and beauty. Lions are the only big cats that live in large groups. Also, they have the loudest roar of any cat, which can be heard for up to five miles!

5.   Places where lions live are coloured green. Despite the nickname King of the jungle, lions do not live in the jungle. They live in flat grassy plains called savannas; they usually have a certain place in the savannas where they like to stay. In ancient times, lions roamed nearly every continent. Today, they can

10. be found across central and southern Africa. There is also a smallpopulation in the Gir forest of India in the continent of Asia.

       Lions have tawny, or yellowish brown, fur. They grow to a length of about 10 feet (3 m) and stand about 4 feet (1.2 m) tall. Male lions are larger than the lionesses (females), weighing as

15. much as five men or about 550 lb (250 kg). The more slender lioness weighs much less than males, about 400 lb (180 kg).

       Adult males can be recognized by the furry mane that runs around the heads and down the neck. For some lions the mane

20. even runs along the belly. There is no other big cat with such a dramatic difference in appearance between males and females. Both lions and lionesses have tufts on the end of their tails, something no other cat has. If you could touch a male lion's tail, you would feel a sharp bone tucked into the tail tuft. One old

25. legend claims that lions would use the tail spur to whip themselves into a frenzy before fighting.

       Lions are the most social cats, living in large groups called prides. Prides are made up of one to three related adult males, along with as many as thirty females and cubs. The females are

30. usually closely related to each other, being a large family of sisters and daughters. Adult males do not do the hunting, but they do serve an important role in the pride. The male lion is much stronger than the female. This makes him an able protector, especially when the females are hunting and the cubs are at risk of marauders, such as hyenas. Male lions use their muscles and fighting skills to guard the land and keep enemies away. Sometimes those enemies are other lions. In prides, cubs are cared for not just by their mothers but by other adult females, as well. Often, one or two lionesses (female lions) will stay with the

40. cubs while the other females hunt. If a cub becomes an orphan,

it is common for it to be cared for by other females who are related to it, perhaps by a lioness who is an aunt or older sister. When young male lions reach the age of one year, they are chased from the prides they are born into by the older male lions.

45.   If the young males leave the pride, they become "rogue" males. They travel alone or may partner with other rogues, perhaps brothers. Having a partner makes it easier for a rogue lion to survive and eventually win a pride of his own. These rogue lions are often found scavenging food killed by smaller

50.   predators, such as hyenas or jackals, which can be chased away. Rogue lions hunt for themselves until they are able to take over a pride of their own!

43.   Why is the title **"King of the Jungle"** unusual ?

A.   ...because lions live in the jungle.
B.   ...because lions live on flat grassy plains.
C.   ...because lions live in zoos.
D.   ...because lions live on farms.
E.   ...because lions are wild animals.

44.   What are young males called when they leave the group of lions ?

A.   cubs   B.   lionesses   C.   rogues
D.   lions   E.   prey

45.   Most lions live

A.   ...in zoos.   B.   ...in India.
C.   ...in Asia.   D.   ...in the jungle.
E.   ...in central and southern Africa.

46.   The flat grassy plains on which lions live are called

A.   ...forests   B.   ...fields   C.   ...savannas
D.   ...jungles   E.   ...continents

47.   From which other animal are young lion cubs at risk ?

A.   ...other cubs   B.   ...lionesses   C.   ...male lions
D.   ...marauders   E.   ...hyenas

10.

48. What happens to young males when they become a year old ?

A. ...they become leaders of the pride.
B. ...they are taught to hunt for themselves.
C. ...they are cared for by their mothers.
D. ...they are chased from their pride.
E. ...they choose to leave their family.

49. The best description of mature lions is

A. loud roar, tawny fur, 3 metres long, 250 Kg in weight.
B. 150 Kg in weight, black coat, 1 metre tall, slender.
C. 5 metres long, 550 Kg in weight, short fur, tame roar.
D. eat grass, 3 metres in length, yellow hair, 100 Kg in weight.
E. meat eater, 2 metres in height, tawny fur, smaller than lionesses.

50. An adult male lion is **different** from an adult lioness by

A. ...the number of cubs he has fathered.
B. ...the amount of food he can find.
C. ...the length of its tail.
D. ...the large furry mane around its head and neck.
E. ...the colour of its fur.

51. To feed the prides of lions the hunting is carried out by

A. ...the cubs   B. ...the male lions
C. ...other animals   D. ...the lionesses
E. ...the native people

52. What is the main responsibility of the adult male lions in a pride ?

A. ...to hunt for food.
B. ...to protect the pride.
C. ...to fight their cubs.
D. ...to fight the lionesses.
E. ...to lead their prides out of the jungle.

53. The word in the first **paragraph** which means the same as **sign** or **representation** is

A. group   B. symbol   C. worshipped
D. beauty   E. major

54. The adverb in **line 48** is

A. these   B. pride   C. survive
D. eventually   E. win

55. **Line 50** has the word **predators**. Predators are

A. ...animals which are eaten by other animals.
B. ...animals which hunt humans.
C. ...animals which are plant-eaters.
D. ...animals that are easily chased away.
E. ...animals which hunt and kill other animals.

General Section

To answer these questions, you may have to think about the passages you have read. Look back at these if you need to. Look also at the Index and Glossary.

56. (a)   An exclamation mark (**!**) is used

A. ...to indicate that a question has been asked.
B. ...to indicate that words have been spoken.
C. ...to indicate that something dramatic has been written.
D. ...to indicate that a sentence has ended.

(b). The words which have the past tense of the verbs **"go"** and **"tear"** are

A. going / torn   B. tore / went
C. gone / tearing   D. teared / goed

57. (a)   Which words in the GLOSSARY are adjectives ?

A. marauders / cleft   B. stimulating / academic
C. rogue / genre   D. fantasy / endeavours

(b). In which part of the Test is there a lot of numerical information ?

A. General section   B. THE LIFE OF BLYTON
C. LAST OF THE PHAIRS   D. KINGS of the JUNGLE

12.

58. (a) Which word in the GLOSSARY means the same as **"lifelike picture of a person"** ?

A. major   B. rogue
C. portrait   D. genre

(b). Which pair of words below have the **correct plurals** ?

A. halfs / echos   B. chefs / heroes
C. valleys / armys   D. pence / tooths

59. (a) Which of the following has **no singular** ?

A. trousers   B. cupfuls
C. drums   D. children

(b). Which pair of words below are **homonymns** ?

A. profit and loss   B. answer and question
C. son-in-law and outlaw   D. higher and hire

60. (a) In which part of the test is there **no mention** of humans ?

A. THE LIFE of BLYTON   B. LAST of the PHAIRS
C. KINGS of the JUNGLE   D. General Section

(b). Some of the words in the INDEX are pronounced as ' **f** ' but are not spelt with an ' **f** '. One of these is

A. LIFE   B. Pharaoh
C. Forsyth   D. Africa

13.

GLOSSARY

minimal------- least possible amount
genre---------- style of literature, art or music
academic----- belonging to education
resiny--------- like the sticky substance (sap) from trees
fantasy---------- imagination, daydream, fictional
endeavours---- attempts, efforts
stimulating--- rousing, exhilarating
portrait------- picture of a person, usually their face
prejudice----- unfair dislike or preference
wryly------------ drily, funny
formidable---- menacing, threatening, daunting
cleft-------------- narrow opening or crack
major---------- greater in number, quality or content
frenzy--------- wild excitement
slender-------- slim, thin, small amount
marauders---- raiding in search of things to steal
rogue---------- dishonest person, rascal, villain
scavenging---- searching among discarded material

INDEX